HOW TO BE A
BIBLE WARRIOR

HOW TO BE A
BIBLE WARRIOR

C. M. MACKENZIE

CF4•K

Dedication:
To four Bible Warriors -
Roderick, William, Hugh and Kenneth Mackenzie

10 9 8 7 6 5 4 3 2 1

© Copyright 2013 Christian Focus Publications
ISBN: 978-1-78191-231-7

Published in 2013 by
Christian Focus Publications,
Geanies House, Fearn, Tain, Ross-shire, IV20 1TW, U.K.

Cover design by Daniel van Straaten
Illustrations by Jeff Anderson
Printed and bound by Nørhaven, Denmark

Scripture quotations are based on The Holy Bible, English Standard Version, copyright © 2001 by Crossway Bibles, a division of Good News Publishers. Used by permission. All rights reserved. ESV Text Edition: 2007.

Contents

WHAT IS A WARRIOR?

Picture this – you go outside one morning and find a time machine on your doorstep. Without thinking you go inside and push the first button you see. While you are saying to yourself, 'That was a silly thing to do,' the time machine takes you back hundreds of years and then spits you out in the past with a sword, a shield and a helmet.

'Great!' you exclaim excitedly as you put them on – just for fun. And then you turn around as a rather loud rumble sounds out from behind you. 'Where is all that dust coming from?' you ask. 'Are those horses in the distance? Did somebody just yell, "Charge!"? Oh no! I'm in a battle,' you gasp.

What should you do next? Should you...

a. Run to find the nearest dragon. Warriors always have a friendly dragon don't they?
b. Run to find the nearest dragon. Warriors need to destroy dangerous dragons don't they?
c. Don't bother with the dragons. There might be a damsel in distress that you could help.

(Damsel is a fancy word for a girl by the way!)

Well if you answered a, b or c – you've got the wrong title. You probably wanted the fairy tale section in the bookshop – but don't worry I won't tell anyone.

And anyway if you really did find yourself a couple of hundred metres away from a charging army – I think the best thing to do would be ...

RUN FOR YOUR LIFE!

However, with all this talk about dragons and damsels let's get one thing straight, the stories in this book are not fairy stories or fiction, but fact.

These Bible Warriors are real. They all fought for the true God, but not all of them shed blood. They weren't perfect either. Some made mistakes, some disobeyed God and some just thought they knew best – when they obviously didn't.

'Hang on a second,' I hear you say. 'This book is called *How to be a Bible Warrior*. How can I be a warrior of any sort if I don't have a sword? Can I have a sword, please, please, pleeaaase?'

No you can't have a sword – well not a metal one anyway. Being a Bible Warrior is not about swords and spears and all that stuff. Being a true Bible Warrior is about fighting against our desire to sin and giving all the praise and glory to the one true God. We are all sinners so this is a battle we all need to fight.

The Bible Warriors we will read about teach us to stand up for the truth and to fight for what is right. We're to be warriors against sin and the devil. We're to cheer on Jesus – the Prince of Peace.

And just because Jesus is called 'The Prince of Peace' don't think that he is a walkover. Jesus is all powerful, or sovereign, but he's called Prince of Peace because he came to bring peace between sinners and God. When he died on the cross instead of sinners he took the punishment for sin and then rose to life again on the third day. Jesus has already defeated sin and death. He is the victor. He has won!

So if the battle has been won what are we fighting for? That is a good question. I think now is the time to run through some basic words.

Battle – A lot of the stories in this book are about actual flesh and blood battles – but the real battle that Christians are fighting is a battle against evil. It's a spiritual battle. In this battle you are either on God's side or on Satan's side. Satan is the enemy of God, a fallen angel, one who is not as powerful as God, but who puts all his energy and evil nature into trying to destroy God's kingdom and God's people. However, he is losing – in fact he has lost – he just wants to keep fighting. He fights by trying to make God's people give in to sin and to stop sinners trusting in Jesus. But remember God is always in control.

Sin – Because Adam and Eve, the first man and woman, disobeyed God (Genesis 3) every human being sins. Sin is when we disobey God. It's when we don't do what he wants us to do and it's when we do what he doesn't want us to do.

Temptation – This is the desire to sin and because human beings are born wanting to sin, it is hard to fight against it. Very often we give in. We need God's strength to fight against sin and temptation.

Do you want to be a Bible Warrior? Well trust in Christ to save you from your sin. And all right then – you can have a sword. All good warriors have a sword but your sword is the Word of God. Plug into the source of all power – God the Father through the Bible and prayer. Now read on to find out more about how you can be a Bible Warrior.

Read more: You can read about Jesus' death and resurrection in Matthew 27:32–28:20; Mark 15:16–16:19; Luke 23–24 and John 19–20

ABRAM TO THE RESCUE

What would you do if one of your relatives was a bit mean to you and then they found themselves in trouble? Would you ...

a. Gloat and say 'Serves them right. I'm not lifting a finger to help them.'

b. Laugh and laugh until you got the hiccups.

c. Sigh, check your diary and say, 'Oh all right then. I'm not doing anything important today.

Well of all three options c is the best but even then I don't think the person who chooses c really wants to be that helpful.

The Warrior we read of in this chapter had his faults. Abram made mistakes but we don't read about him dragging his feet when one day he had to rescue his nephew Lot. Let's find out how Lot got into trouble in the first place.

It all started with two large flocks of sheep. Abram and his nephew, Lot, had both been blessed by God. They were wealthy and their flocks were doing well. With so many sheep, Abram and Lot had to employ herdsmen and unfortunately both groups of men felt they were in competition with each other. Abram's herdsmen wanted the best grass and water for Abram's sheep. Lot's herdsmen thought that Lot's sheep should have the best. This led to some squabbles between the two groups.

Abram's men would say 'Move over! It should be Abram's sheep that get the water first.'

Lot's men would reply, 'Says who? That's not fair. Our sheep are thirstier than yours.'

'They look fine to us,' Abram's men would snap back. 'Our Master is more important than yours anyway.'

'Oh no he isn't,' was the reply. 'Oh yes he is,' was the next reply.

Then before long the fists were out and the men were hitting and punching each other. It would happen every time Lot and Abram's herdsmen got together to feed and water the sheep. Abram and Lot heard about it and knew that something had to be done.

As they travelled through foreign lands, Abram knew that it was important to keep his family on good terms with each other.

FACT FILE

Abram's father, Terah, had taken his family from Ur of the Chaldeans in order to go to the land of Canaan. Abram and his wife Sarai and Terah's grandson, Lot went too. After Terah's death, God promised Abram that he would make a great nation out of his descendants; even though Abram and his wife Sarai had no son to carry on the family name, not even a single child.

Abram said to Lot, 'Let there be no strife between you and me, and between your herdsmen and my herdsmen, for we are kinsmen.'

Then Abram pointed to the land around them, 'Separate yourself from me. If you take the left hand then I will go to the right or if you take the right hand then I will go to the left.'

This seemed a good idea to Lot when he saw that the Jordan Valley to the East was lush and green with lots of good water. 'I'll go there,' he announced; taking the best land for himself.

Perhaps Abram felt a little down-hearted and hard done by. He had given his nephew, Lot, the first choice – the polite thing to do – but now this meant that Abram's flocks could not feed on the rich pasture of the Jordan valley. However, just after this took place, God came to Abram with a message.

'Lift up your eyes and look from the place where you are, northward and southward and eastward and westward, for all the land that you see I will give to you and to your offspring forever.'

So Abram moved his tent and came and settled by the Oaks of Mamre and there he built an altar to the Lord.

Lot meanwhile must have thought he'd made a really good choice. However, he had chosen to ignore that his new home was in the middle of considerable unrest and that the people he would be living alongside did what was evil in the eyes of the Lord God.

In this area there were four kings fighting against five other kings. The four kings were Chedorlaomer, King of Elam; Tidal King of Goyim; Amraphel King of Shinar and Arioch King of Ellasar.

These four kings defeated the five kings of Sodom and Gomorrah. The kings of Sodom and Gomorrah fled to the hill country leaving behind all their wealth and possessions for the enemy. You can read about this in Genesis 14.

Lot was in the wrong place at the wrong time. The four victorious kings kidnapped him and took all his possessions. What he'd thought was a good decision – to move to this rich fertile land – had turned out to be rather unwise.

However, someone from Lot's camp managed to escape and fled to Abram to tell him all that had happened. Abram immediately mustered his troops. He led his trained men forward, those who had been born in his house, 318 of them in total. And he went off in hot pursuit as far as the area of Dan.

The four kings who had defeated the five kings of Sodom and Gomorrah would surely be able to get the better of one wandering rancher and his men. But Abram divided his forces so that his men fought the four kings and their troops day and night. Abram's servants defeated Chedorlaomer and the others and sent them packing. They fled to Hobah, north of Damascus.

Abram then returned with all the stolen possessions, and also brought back Lot with his possessions, and the women and the people.

The King of Sodom was delighted and said to Abram, 'Let the people come back with me but help yourself to the possessions.'

Abram then said a very wise thing, 'I have lifted my hand to the LORD, God Most High, Possessor of heaven and earth, that I would not take a thread or sandal strap or anything that is yours, lest you should say, "I have made Abram rich."'

Abram took nothing that day except what his men had eaten and what was due to his men for their fighting in the battle.

Abram didn't want the wicked king of Sodom to get the glory that belonged to God.

Then God came to Abram with another message. 'Fear not Abram. I am your shield; your reward shall be very great ... Look toward the heaven and number the stars if you are able to number them. So shall your offspring be.'

And even though Abram had no son, he still believed the Lord and God counted it to him as righteousness.

WARRIOR WAYS

Often in stories of battles we hear of how soldiers would help themselves to treasure after they had won the battle. This was also called spoils or plunder. Abram didn't help himself to any spoils however. There was someone more important in his mind – the Lord God. When he speaks to the King of Sodom he calls God 'Creator of Heaven and Earth'. He's telling this unbelieving king that everything he owns actually belongs to God first.

It is the same with you. Every good and perfect gift has been given to you by God. Even if you believe in him or not, trust in him or not, your breath, your life, everything you eat and drink has been graciously given to you by God. And if you trust in the Lord Jesus Christ and have had your sins forgiven – you have been given the most perfect gift that there has ever been – the gift of salvation.

THINK ABOUT JESUS

Abram received many blessings from God, but in Genesis chapter 12, God said something very special about how Abram would be a blessing.

'In you all the nations of the earth shall be blessed.'

How would Abram bless all the nations of the earth? Well, it wasn't Abram but someone who was born into Abram's family line – Jesus Christ. And it is by dying on the cross in the place of sinners that Jesus has blessed the whole world.

Read more: You can read more about Abram in Genesis 12–15.

UNUSUAL VICTORIES

What would you do if you were about to fight an important battle? Would you:

a. Send in a choir as your first defence?

b. Choose an elderly man as your back up?

c. Start off with 32,000 men and then send most of them home?

You are probably thinking, where's the fourth option? I don't like the look of any of these. Well in one way you're right. If you were going out to a battle and wanting to win it, normally you wouldn't choose a, b or c.

But in the next three stories each of these options was chosen.

Story 1: The Choir

This battle was between the king, Jehoshaphat, and some enemy tribes, the Moabites, the Ammonites and the Meunites. Jehoshaphat was the King of Judah and a direct descendant of one of Israel's greatest kings, King David.

I suppose we need a bit of a history lesson here. David was the second King of Israel and after him came his son, Solomon. When Solomon died, his son, Rehoboam, became king and it was during his reign that the country of Israel split in two. So from that point on in the history of the Bible, where there had been one country and one king, there were now two.

The land of Israel was ruled by Jeroboam, a man who had been a servant of Solomon. The tribe of Judah remained loyal to the descendants of David and they were ruled over by Rehoboam and his descendants who came after him.

When Rehoboam died, his son Abijam reigned in his place. When Abijam died, his son Asa reigned in his place. Asa did what was right in the eyes of the Lord. And when Asa died, his son Jehoshaphat reigned in his place. And he was the man who sent a choir into the battle as his first defence ... let's find out about that, shall we?

Jehoshaphat's father had been a good example to him. And he also obeyed the Lord's commandments. He built up the defences of the land of Judah and did not worship false gods. The land of Israel, however, was ruled over by King Ahab who had been led into worshiping idols by his wicked wife, Jezebel.

Jehoshaphat, however, was courageous in the ways of the Lord and attempted to get rid of the idols from the land of Judah. He even sent out the priests to go around the land teaching the people about God.

He didn't always make good decisions though. Once he made an alliance with King Ahab and they went into battle, despite the fact that the prophet Micaiah had warned them that the battle would go against them. When King Ahab was killed by an arrow shot, Jehoshaphat managed to escape to his house in Jerusalem where a message from God was waiting for him.

The message was, 'Why are you helping the wicked and showing love to those who hate the LORD? God is angry with you. Nevertheless, some good is found in you, for you destroyed the idols and set your heart to seek God.'

Jehoshaphat then returned to following God's ways so that when the enemy tribes came up against him, he knew what he had to do. Jehoshaphat asked the Lord God for help.

The people, including all the women and the children and the little babies, gathered together and Jehoshaphat prayed before the Lord, 'O LORD, God of our fathers, are you not God in heaven? You rule over all the kingdoms of the nations. In your hand are power and might, so that none is able to withstand you. And now behold the men of Ammon and Moab and Mount Seir are coming to drive us out of your possessions which you have given us to inherit. O God, will you not execute judgment on them? For we are powerless against this great horde that is coming against us. We do not know what to do, but our eyes are on you.'

At that point the Spirit of the Lord came down upon a man named Jahaziel, a Levite – someone who was a servant of God in the temple. He said, 'Listen all Judah and inhabitants of Jerusalem and King Jehoshaphat: The Lord says to you, "Do not be afraid and do not be dismayed at this great horde, for the battle is not yours but God's. Tomorrow, go down against them ... You will not need to fight in this battle. Stand firm, hold your position, and see the salvation of the Lord on your behalf, O Judah and Jerusalem. Do not be afraid and do not be dismayed. Tomorrow go out against them, and the Lord will be with you."'

Then Jehoshaphat bowed down and all Judah and the inhabitants of Jerusalem fell down before the Lord. The Levites stood up to praise the Lord, the God of Israel, with a very loud voice.

The next day, before they went into battle, Jehoshaphat declared to the people, 'Believe in

28

the LORD your God and you will be established; believe his prophets and you will succeed.'

Then after he had sought some advice, he appointed those who were to sing to the Lord and praise him as they went before the army.

The words the choir sang were, 'Give thanks to the LORD, for his steadfast love endures for ever.'

The choir set off in front of the army and when they arrived at the battlefield they discovered that their enemies had in fact destroyed each other. Dead bodies were everywhere. Jehoshaphat and his army didn't even have to lift their swords. God's Word had been true. 'You will not need to fight this battle. The battle is not yours, but God's.'

Story 2: The Elderly Man

So what about the elderly man? Well, long before Israel had a king, God promised them that they would have a land of their own, but at that time the Israelites were in fact slaves to the Egyptians. You can read about this in the first few chapters of Exodus in the Old Testament.

Although the Israelite people were slaves of the Egyptians, God had a plan to free them and that plan involved a baby.

This little boy was born into an Israelite family at a very dangerous time. All young Israelite boys were in danger of being killed by the soldiers of the Egyptian ruler, Pharaoh. But one lad's mother hatched a plan. She hid him in a waterproof basket and placed it by the river Nile, amongst some bulrushes. His sister was left to keep an eye on him. However, even though the baby was well hidden, Pharaoh's daughter discovered him. She decided to keep the baby for herself. The baby's sister saw an opportunity and seized it. Dashing up to the princess, she suggested that it would be a good idea to find a nurse to look after the baby and that she knew just the right person. The princess agreed and the baby, who was called Moses, was given back to his real mother to look after. She was even given some wages for doing the job. So Moses was brought up as the son of Pharaoh's daughter, but he was also brought up in a loving, godly family. His own family.

The boy grew up, eventually leaving the power and privilege of Pharaoh's palace to take his position as leader of the Israelite people. It was a struggle to get Pharaoh to set the slaves free. God sent plagues – locusts, hail, boils, and other horrible events.

The last and final plague was when the angel of death came over the land and the first born of every Egyptian family died. The Israelites were told to paint the door posts and lintels of their homes with the blood of a lamb. When the angel of death saw that blood, he would pass over the homes and the Israelite families would be saved.

After that terrible plague, Pharaoh let the Israelites go and they set off on what would be a long journey to the land God had promised them. There were many dangers along the road such as enemy tribes, one of which was the Amalekites.

When this tribe attacked the Israelites, Moses turned to his assistant Joshua and said, 'Choose for us men, and go out and fight against Amalek. Tomorrow I will stand on the top of the hill with the staff of God in my hand.'

Joshua did as Moses said and fought against Amalek while Moses, his brother Aaron and Hur went up to the top of the hill.

They noticed that whenever Moses held up his hands, Israel would win the battle, but whenever he lowered his hands, Israel began to lose.

It became apparent that Moses was beginning to get very tired. His arms began to get lower and lower. The men who were with him got a large stone for him to sit and rest upon. And then Aaron took one arm and Hur the other and held Moses' arms up until the sun had set and Joshua had totally routed Amalek with the sword.

The Lord then said to Moses, 'Write this as a memorial in a book and recite it in the ears of Joshua, that I will utterly blot out the memory of Amalek from under heaven.'

Moses then built an altar and called it, 'The Lord is my banner'.

FACT FILE

Even today many regiments have flags or banners that they take into battle with them. A banner was supposed to identify a group of people – like a badge or a logo might do today. The banner would tell the enemy to watch out. When the banner or flag was flying high, the people who carried it were confident. The enemy would see it and would be afraid. When Moses referred to God as his banner, he was saying that God was his confidence, that he trusted in him. He was making sure that God's enemies knew that God was his defence, that the Lord God went before his people and that God's enemies had better watch out!

Story 3: 300 Men

Three hundred men are hardly enough to fight a massive army? Are they? In fact the commander of this particular battle wasn't that promising either. He wasn't that brave or strong. But God had chosen him. Gideon was the Lord's choice and he was the best choice.

The Lord sent an angel to Gideon to tell him of his plans. 'The LORD is with you O mighty man of valour.'

What would you do if an angel appeared and said that to you? Would you start an argument? Well, Gideon tried to.

He started to complain about the Midianites, an enemy tribe who were making things really difficult for the Israelites. He continued to complain about all the troubles. 'Where are all God's wonderful actions that our parents kept telling us about?'

The angel of the Lord turned to Gideon and said, 'Go in this might of yours and save Israel from the hand of Midian; do not I send you?'

Gideon couldn't understand this. 'How can I save Israel? Behold my family is the weakest in our whole tribe and I'm the most unimportant person in my whole family?'

Then the Lord said to him, 'I will be with you.'

Still Gideon wasn't convinced. He decided that he wanted a special sign from God. Speaking to an angel wasn't good enough for Gideon! He ran to his house, got a young goat, some cakes and flour. He put meat in a basket and some broth in a pot and presented them as an offering to the Lord. The angel of God told Gideon to put the meat and cakes on a rock and to pour the broth over them. Gideon did this and then the angel of the Lord took a staff that was in his hand and touched the food with the tip of it. Fire sprang up and consumed all the meat and the cakes and then the angel of the Lord vanished.

Gideon realised just then that he hadn't just met an ordinary angel but that he had met the Angel of the Lord face to face. He was terrified, but God said to him, 'Peace be to you. Do not fear. You shall not die.'

That night Gideon was given his first task by the Lord. He was to take his father's two bulls and pull down the altar that his father had built to false gods. In its place, Gideon was to build an altar to the one true God.

Gideon did this with ten of his servants, but he was too afraid to do it during the day in case his family saw him, so he did it at night instead.

And he still wasn't sure that God was really going to do what he had said. He said to God, 'If you are really going to save Israel through me

as you have said, I'm going to put this sheep's fleece on the barn floor. In the morning if there is dew on the fleece and it is dry all around on the ground, then I shall know that you will save Israel by my hand as you have said.'

The next morning Gideon got up early and squeezed the fleece – there was enough dew to fill a bowl with water.

Then Gideon said, 'Please let me test just once more with the fleece. Let it be dry on the fleece only and all the ground around be wet with dew.'

God did exactly that. The next day the fleece was dry and all the ground was wet. So Gideon and the Israelite army got ready to attack the Midianites.

But then God said something that must have sounded strange, 'The people with you are too many. When you defeat the Midianites, Israel will boast over me, "My own hand has saved me." So tell the people that whoever is fearful can return home.'

Twenty-two thousand of the people returned and ten thousand people were left. God said that was still too many. 'Take them down to the water,' he told Gideon. 'Everyone who laps the water with his tongue as a dog laps, put them to one side. Those who kneel down to drink – put to the other side.'

The number of men who lapped the water was 300. All the rest knelt down to drink.

God said to Gideon, 'With the 300 men who lapped I will save you and give the Midianites into your hand. Let all the others go home.'

That night the Lord said to Gideon, 'I have given the Midianite camp into your hand, but if you're afraid, go down with your servant Purah and you shall hear what they say and your hands will be strengthened.'

So Gideon and his servant went down to the Midianite camp and overheard an interesting conversation between two soldiers. One soldier had had a dream and he was sure it must mean something.

'Behold I dreamed a dream about a cake of barley bread that tumbled into the camp of Midian and came into the tent and struck it so that it fell and turned the tent upside down.'

The soldier's friend replied, 'That's the sword of Gideon the son of Joash, a man of Israel; God has given into his hand Midian and all the camp.'

As soon as Gideon heard this, he worshipped the Lord. He then divided the 300 men into three groups and gave them all trumpets and empty jars with torches inside the jars.

Gideon then said to them, 'Look at me and do what I do. When I come to the outskirts of the camp and blow the trumpet, I and all who are with me, then blow your trumpets also on every side of the camp and shout, 'A sword for the LORD and for Gideon.'

So Gideon and the men came to the outskirts of the camp just when the night watch had begun. They blew their trumpets and smashed the jars, and the two other groups did exactly the same. They held up their torches and cried out, 'A sword for the LORD and for Gideon.'

All the Midianite army cried out and fled. They even started fighting each other. Quite a victory for such a small army you might say? But remember who the real victor was! The Lord God won this battle.

WARRIOR WAYS

So what do we learn from these three stories? They all teach us that when we are struggling with temptation, fighting against sin, facing up to troubles in our life, it is God that we should turn to for help. The Lord God is our strength. He has all power. When you are struggling, trust in him and praise him, for our Lord and Saviour is truly good, no matter what is going on in our life. And then when things are going well, trust in him then too and give him praise and all the glory.

THINK ABOUT JESUS

Jesus' life and death is a victory – though it might not have appeared that way to the people who saw Jesus' body hanging from the cross. But when Jesus died on the cross it was not because he had unfortunately been arrested by wicked men and it had all gone wrong. He suffered and died on the cross because it was God the Father's plan. Jesus would suffer and die on the cross and at the same time take the punishment for sin. Jesus who had never sinned in his life became sin instead of sinners. He was willing to take this sin, so that when God the Father looked on his Son and saw that sin, Jesus would be punished instead. Jesus did that for sinners like us.

Then three days later, Jesus rose from the dead. Sin was defeated on the cross and at the tomb. Jesus' death was not a defeat, it was a victory. Jesus died for sinners, rose again for sinners and will take forgiven sinners to heaven to be with him – forever.

Read more: You can read about Jehoshaphat in 2 Chronicles 20, Moses and the Amalekites in Exodus 17:8-16, Gideon and the 300 men in Judges 7.

FROM SHEPHERD BOY TO KING

An important thing for a warrior is the king you are fighting for. So if you were to choose a king, what characteristics do you think would make a good one?

Would you want him to be:

a. The most handsome?

b. The tallest?

c. Handy with a catapult?

Quite a few people think physical appearance is important. They don't want an ugly king. Others think it's important to be tall. They don't want a tiny king. Others think you need someone who is tough and strong and a good fighter. What we're going to find out in this chapter is that God disagrees with all of them.

The young shepherd boy, David, would not have been anyone's first choice for king, especially when he was standing alongside his seven other brothers. He was good with a catapult and he was considered handsome, but when you have seven older brothers, some people ignore you. However, God doesn't.

The prophet Samuel was told by the Lord one day that he was no longer happy with Saul as king. Saul had turned away from God and so God no longer wanted him to rule Israel.

The Lord God told Samuel to go and visit Jesse the Bethlehemite because the new king would be found amongst his sons.

'You will anoint for me him who I declare to you.'

Samuel did as the Lord commanded and came to Bethlehem to perform a sacrifice to the Lord which Jesse and his sons were to attend.

When they came, Samuel looked at the oldest son, Eliab, and thought, 'Surely that is the LORD's anointed.' But the LORD said, 'Do not look at his appearance or at how tall he is, because I have rejected him. For the LORD sees not as man sees: man looks on the outward appearance, but the LORD looks on the heart.'

Then Jesse called all his other sons to come before Samuel, but the Lord had chosen none of them.

Samuel must have been puzzled. He turned to Jesse and asked, 'Are all your sons here?'

Jesse replied, 'There's the youngest, but he is in the fields looking after the sheep.'

'Send for him,' Samuel demanded. 'For we will not proceed with the sacrifice until he is here.' So David, the youngest of Jesse's sons, was sent for.

When David arrived at the festivities, he was anointed king in front of his father and all his brothers and from that day on, the Spirit of the Lord was on David.

It wasn't long before David was given the opportunity to prove that it's not looks, nor height nor skills that are important – it is God.

The Philistines, you see, were one of Israel's most bitter enemies and they had an impressive warrior in their midst called Goliath. He was massive – about 2.76 metres tall and counting. The Bible gives his measurements as being a span taller than six cubits and a cubit was about 46 centimetres ... so you can work it out.

He was armed to the hilt – helmet of bronze; coat of mail; bronze armour on his legs; a javelin slung between his shoulders – he also had a spear – and a shield which was carried for him by someone else.

When the Philistines and the Israelites were facing each other in battle one day, everything had ground to a halt. The two armies were poised to fight, but no one was willing to take the first step. The Philistine giant, Goliath, kept challenging the Israelites to send out their best fighters to fight him, but no one from the Israelite camp was willing to risk it.

Now David was too young to be in the army, but his brothers had joined up. His father Jesse wanted to find out how the battle was going so he sent David to the army camp. 'Take for your brothers this parched grain and these ten loaves. Also take these ten cheeses to give to their commander. See if your brothers are well and bring me some news back.'

So David set off for the Valley of Elah where the fighting was taking place against the Philistines. When David arrived, the Philistine giant, Goliath, had just come out onto the battlefield, yelling his usual insults against the army of the Lord.

David was angry as he heard the abuse that Goliath hurled at the Israelite camp. 'Who is this Philistine that he should defy the armies of the living God?'

With fighting talk like that, it's no surprise that eventually David found his way to the presence of King Saul. David said to the king that he would fight the Philistine. Saul wasn't so sure. 'You are not able to go against this Philistine for you are too young and Goliath has been a man of war since his youth.'

But David replied, 'Your servant has looked after sheep for his father. And when a lion or a bear came to take a lamb from the flock, I would go after him and strike him and deliver the lamb from its mouth. And if it arose against me, I would catch it by its fur and strike it and kill it.

'This Philistine shall be like one of those wild animals, for he has defied the armies of the Living God. The LORD who has delivered me from the paw of the lion and the bear will deliver me from the hand of this Philistine.'

Saul responded, 'Go, and the LORD be with you.'

So David went out to face the giant Goliath armed only with a catapult and five smooth stones. But Goliath didn't think that David was a worthy opponent.

'Come to me,' he snarled, 'and I will give your flesh to the birds of the air and the beasts of the field.'

David looked him in the eye and declared, 'You come to me with a spear and a javelin, but I come to you in the name of the LORD of hosts, the God of the armies of Israel whom you have defied. This day the LORD will deliver you into my hand, and I will strike you down and cut off your head. And I will give the dead bodies of the host of the Philistines this day to the birds of the air and to the wild beasts of the earth, so that all the world may know that there is a God in Israel and that all this assembly may know that the LORD saves not with sword and spear – for the battle is the LORD's and he will give you into our hand.'

Goliath arose to come against David, but David ran quickly towards the battle line to face him. David put his hand in his bag and took out a stone and slung it and struck the Philistine in the forehead.

Goliath fell flat onto the ground – dead.

Then David ran to Goliath's body, took the Philistine's sword and cut off his head with it.

As soon as the Philistines saw what had happened, they ran for their lives.

The shepherd boy who wasn't as good looking as his older brother, and who certainly wasn't as tall as Goliath and who only had a catapult to fight this giant – was the winner – not because of his strength or skill, but because the battle belonged to the Lord God. It was David's God who was the victor that day.

WARRIOR WAYS

God used David to fight his battle so that we who read his word many years later will see that it's not about how great David was but it's about how great God is. God uses people to make his kingdom bigger, but it should never be about us. It should always be about God. Give him the glory.

THINK ABOUT JESUS

David was a great fighter but there was someone in his family tree who was far greater than him. David was a sinner. Though he fought valiantly, he didn't always mange to defeat sin and temptation. But the Lord Jesus Christ is a descendant of David and he totally crushed the power of sin – and even defeated death.

Read more: You can read about David and Goliath in 1 Samuel 17.

THREE OF DAVID'S MIGHTY MEN

When you see an adventure movie on T.V., there's usually a hero who saves the day. Which of the following do you think would make a really good movie?

a. A hero rescues a baby from a burning building.

b. A heroine defeats some terrorists on a plane.

c. A hero and a heroine stop a super criminal from launching a nuclear rocket.

d. Several heroes rush to a nearby town to get some fresh water.

Okay I know you're all saying 'What? D's a bit lame isn't it?'

But really that's what the heroes of this story did – there were three of them.

1. Josheb-basshebeth
2. Eleazar the son of Dodo
3. Shammah the son of Agee

It's a lot easier to say 'My name is Bond, James Bond' than say 'My name is Josheb-basshebeth' ... but these guys make James Bond look like a sissy. Let's read the stats on the Big Three.

Josheb-basshebeth. He belonged to a family group called Tahchemon. He was the chief of the three mighty men. The battle he was best known for was one when he wielded his spear against eight hundred men and killed all of them.

The next is Eleazar. He fought against the Philistines even when the men of Israel withdrew. He rose and struck down the Philistines until his hand was weary and was almost stuck to his sword.

Then we've got Shammah. He was the last man facing the Philistines in a field of lentils. Everyone else had fled. But he took his stand and defended that plot and struck down the Philistines.

These three mighty men joined David one day at the cave of Adullam. David was fleeing from the jealous anger of King Saul. The cave of Adullam was a refuge for David and the people who were flocking to him for protection. David's family and anyone else who was in distress went there. David became their captain – and the number of fighting men amounted to about 400.

When the three mighty men came to Adullam, it was harvest time. There were Philistines camped at Bethlehem, David's home, and he was beginning to feel a bit homesick because he said, 'Oh, that someone would give me water to drink from the well of Bethlehem that is by the gate!'

As soon as he'd said it, the three mighty men set off.

Can you picture it – these three warriors storming the Philistine fort at Bethlehem, breaking through their ranks and charging up to the well just beyond the gate. Two of them were probably using any weapon they could set their hands on while the other was drawing the water from the well as quickly as he could. There would have been a lot of noise as the Philistines raised the alarm. Maybe one or two of the mighty warriors were wounded in the struggle. But they all made it out alive and returned to David at the Cave of Adullam to present him with the gift of the water he had longed for.

David was greatly humbled by the danger they had put themselves in. They had been willing to risk their lives to fulfil their captain's wish. David could not bring himself to drink the water. So he poured it out as an offering to the Lord. 'Far be it from me,' he said, 'O LORD, that I should do this. Shall I drink the blood of the men who went at the risk of their lives?'

WARRIOR WAYS

Each of these three mighty men has bravery written all over him. They are tough, strong, and know what to do in a fight. But twice you read the following words in their story, 'The LORD brought about a great victory'. How easy it would have been for these three men to bask in the glory of victory. They could really have milked that situation. 'Look at what we've done. We're real heroes. Everyone should want to be us and look up to us and – fetch me some dinner and clean my sword while you're at it.' But no – they give the glory to God.

When things go well for you, do you think, 'Well done me!' When someone says, 'Good job,' do you smile to yourself and think 'Too right'?

When things go well – you should thank God and praise him. When someone compliments you, accept that compliment graciously and give the glory to God. 'Yes, thank you. I enjoyed doing that project. I'm so glad God helped me.'

'Winning that race was great. But it was God who helped me. He gave me the strength.'

Giving glory to God is an important part of being a Bible Warrior.

THINK ABOUT JESUS

Now let's think about the ultimate hero. He was sent on an extraordinary mission, God's mission to save the world.

Jesus Christ not only risked his life – he gave it completely so that sinners like us could be saved and live for ever. He died so that we could live. He took the punishment for sin so that sinners who turn away from their sin and turn to God can be cleansed from their sin and the guilt of their sin and be given a life forever in heaven.

What a sacrifice! A much greater sacrifice than the three mighty men. David didn't feel worthy to accept their sacrifice. But Jesus' sacrifice is a sacrifice that you must accept. That's the whole point of it – Jesus sacrificed himself for others. He wants you to come to him and say, 'Thank you Lord Jesus for what you have done. I need your forgiveness, I need your salvation. I accept it as a free gift from God.'

Read more: You can read about David's Three Mighty Men in 2 Samuel 23: 8-17

JOSHUA AND THE BATTLE OF JERICHO

Imagine what your all-time favourite fantasy weapon would be. I've imagined a few - maybe one of them is the same as yours?

a. A telepathic-magnetic-rocket that zones in on untidy bedrooms while turning back time so all bedrooms are clean before anyone is asked to tidy them in the first place ... now that's what I call fantasy!

b. A super-sonic-lazer that blitzes disease and neutralises pain. Now someone might invent that in the future which would be cool.

c. An invisible bionic net that you can hang over a safe or treasure chest and as soon as a robber touches it he is stuck like glue and can't move an inch until the police arrive. I think I might have seen that in a movie once.

These are not your typical spears and arrows or guns are they? They're still weapons though as they are things that I've imagined would be good at attacking things like dirt, disease and robbers. I'm sure you've thought about some other interesting ideas.

By any chance did you think that rams' horns might make a good weapon?

'Rams' horns? What would I do with a ram's horn?' you ask.

Well, Joshua and his army used them as rather effective weapons because God told them to. Let's do a little background information to this story – you're going to need it.

Who is Joshua?

Well, he was an Israelite. His father's name was Nun. He was most likely born into slavery in Egypt, but sometime after Pharaoh's edict that all the Israelite children should be massacred.

What did Joshua do?

He was Moses' assistant and after Moses' death he became the Israelite leader.

Who are the Israelites?

They are the descendants of Abram (or Abraham as he was later called), Isaac and Jacob. Jacob and his family went to live in Egypt after one of Jacob's sons, Joseph, became second in command to Pharaoh. Many years later though a new Pharaoh was in charge and he enslaved the Israelites.

Who was Moses?

Moses was a boy born into an Israelite family at a time when Pharaoh was killing all the Israelite boys. Moses, however, was saved from death by the plan of God. Go back to pages 30-31 to find out how that happened. Moses eventually became the leader of the Israelites.

Then what?

Eventually the Israelites were set free and travelled to the land that God had promised them. Moses was their leader, and Joshua his assistant. When they arrived at the promised land, spies were sent in to scout out the land and the people living there. Joshua was one of those spies with his friend Caleb. When they returned, Joshua and Caleb, gave a good report. But the people choose to believe the other scary reports they'd heard.

'There are giants there. We aren't strong enough to defeat these people.'

The people were too scared to go into the land that God had promised to them. They didn't trust God. Joshua, Caleb and Moses pleaded with the people to trust and obey the Lord, but they would not. So the people wandered in the wilderness for forty years until all the adults who had refused to go into the promised land of Canaan, had died. Their children would now possess the land instead of them. The only two adults, from that older

generation, who entered the promised land were Joshua and Caleb. Not even Moses was allowed to go to the land God had promised. He only saw it from a distance before he died. It would be Joshua who would lead the people from now on.

God instructed the people of Israel to 'Rise up, set out on your journey ... This day I will begin to put the dread and fear of you on the peoples who are under the whole heaven who shall hear about you and shall tremble and be in anguish because of you.'

And the news about God's people spread. The foreign tribes who did not worship the Lord had heard about the battles the Israelites had already fought. The Lord's great power was striking fear into the hearts of these people who did not worship the one true God.

Even the news about how God had delivered these people from slavery in Egypt, had made its way to the city of Jericho. So when Joshua and the Israelites arrived at the River Jordan, the people of Jericho looked anxiously on to see what would happen.

God arranged it so that his people crossed the River Jordan on dry land. Another miracle! Another victory. Jericho was terrified.

When the Israelite army arrived outside Jericho, they would have seen a strong fortification. The walls were huge and well defended. No one was going in and no one was going out. This type of warfare is called a siege.

Then the Lord said to Joshua, 'See I have given Jericho into your hand with its king and mighty men of valour. March round the city, all the men of war going round the city once. Do this for six days. Seven priests shall bear seven trumpets of rams' horns before the ark. On the seventh day you shall march round the city seven times and the priests shall blow the trumpets. And when they make a loud blast with the ram's horn, when you hear the sound of the trumpet then all the people shall shout with a great shout and the wall of the city shall fall down flat, and the people shall go up everyone straight before him.'

Joshua passed on these commands to the people. So every day, for six days, the priests marched round the city once, while the trumpets blew continually. On the seventh day they all rose early and marched around the city in the same way, but this time they marched round seven times. And at the seventh time, when the priests had blown their trumpets Joshua said to the people, 'Shout for the LORD has given you the city. But keep yourselves from the things that God has told you must be destroyed. All the silver and gold and every vessel of bronze and iron should go the treasury of the Lord.'

So the people shouted and trumpets were blown and the wall fell flat so that the people entered the city and captured it.

What a victory God gave Joshua and the Israelites. They certainly couldn't have done it without him.

WARRIOR WAYS

So the Israelites did indeed fight with rams' horns, but it was because of God's power that the Israelites defeated their enemy. I wonder how the people of Jericho felt when they saw the advancing army? They probably felt very scared. But maybe they began to feel differently when they saw the Israelites marching around their city, blowing horns. A brass band isn't usually something to be afraid of. Maybe the people of Jericho started to laugh. They certainly didn't expect their walls to simply collapse. They would have been confident that they were safe behind

these walls. No army had broken through before. But then none of the previous armies had God on their side. When you look at the battles you have to face in your life – remember God. Remember that there is no one who has, or ever will defeat him. He is all-powerful. Start your day with God's Word. The Bible describes it as a sword – a sharp two-edged sword. In Bible times a two-edged sword was a fierce weapon. God's Word – the Bible – is the weapon you need to fight against temptation. It's the weapon you need to fight against people who tell you lies about God and his Word. It's the weapon you need to give you strength to face any problem or difficulty that comes your way. Take God's Word and use it – memorise it so that during those times when you can't stop and read an actual Bible, you can recall what God's Word says.

THINK ABOUT JESUS

Did you know that the story of Joshua has an amazing link to the story of Jesus? Before the Israelites crossed the Jordan and surrounded the city, some spies were sent in to check things out. They hid in the house of a woman named Rahab. But the King of Jericho heard a rumour they were there and sent some soldiers.

Rahab protected the men by hiding them under a pile of flax on the roof of her home. She sent the king's soldiers off in the wrong direction. For Rahab's bravery the two spies promised that she and anyone in her home would be protected when the Israelite army attacked. All she had to do was tie a scarlet cord to her window. Everyone inside the house would be safe.

This was what happened. When the walls of Jericho fell, Rahab's home was safe. Rahab joined with the Israelite people and married a man called Salmon. They had a son called Boaz, who became the father of Obed, who was the father of Jesse, who was the father of King David. And if you look in Matthew 1:5, you will see that Rahab is actually in the family tree of Jesus himself. She is one of his ancestors. Isn't it amazing that she gets mentioned there? She was a foreign woman, who didn't really have a good reputation – but she is honoured with the privilege of being in the family tree of Jesus Christ. You too can be part of Christ's family – God's family – by trusting in him to save you from sin. We are all guilty of sin and in need of salvation. But we can be given this amazing, undeserved, privilege of being in the eternal family of God by believing in Jesus Christ.

Read more: You can read about the Battle of Jericho in Joshua 6.

THE BATTLE OF AI

Armies don't like to spend much time remembering their defeats. What do you think are the most likely reasons for an army to be defeated anyway?

a. Their enemy is bigger than them?

b. Their enemy is stronger than them?

c. They didn't listen to the instructions given to them in their previous battle?

Hmmm ... Well usually it is the bigger and stronger army that wins the day, but sometimes the outcome is different as is the case with the battle we are going to read about now ...

The battle of Jericho had been a great success for Joshua and the Israelite army. They had obeyed God by marching around the city walls and blowing the trumpets just as God had told them to, but there had been other instructions that some of the Israelites had not listened to. God had warned them if they disregarded these commands, they would have to be punished.

Even though the Israelites had had a successful battle at Jericho, they still had quite a bit of ground to cover before they captured the whole of the promised land for themselves. They needed to keep fighting and the next place was a rather small town of Ai.

Joshua asked some of his men to spy on the land round about Ai which was near Beth-Aven, East of Bethel.

The men returned with a favourable report. 'This battle will be easy,' they said. 'It's not worth our while sending the whole army. All we need is three thousand men. The people in Ai are few. They won't cause us much trouble.'

So 3,000 men went up to fight Ai but it didn't work out as planned. The Israelite men, all 3,000 of them, took to their heels and fled. Instead of obliterating Ai as they had planned, the Ai forces killed thirty-six Israelites and chased their troops as far as Shebarim.

The Israelite people were terrified. Their knees became like jelly. They lost all their confidence. Joshua was so upset. He tore his clothes in anguish and fell down on his face before the ark of the Lord.

'Alas, O Lᴏʀᴅ God, why have you brought us over the Jordan to give us into the hands of the Amorites, to destroy us? Israel has fled before her enemies! The inhabitants of this land will hear of this defeat and will surround us and destroy us. And what will you do for your great name?'

God then said to Joshua, 'Get up! Why have you fallen on your face? Israel has sinned. They have broken the covenant that I commanded them.'

FACT FILE

A Covenant is a special promise. The Bible mentions several of them. Sometimes God makes the covenant himself, sometimes it is made by God and man, sometimes it is made between human beings themselves.

This covenant that God reminded Joshua about was one that was also a command from God. He had told the Israelites that after they had defeated the city of Jericho, they were to promise not to touch the things that were to be destroyed or that were to be placed in the Lord's treasury.

If the Israelite people did not obey this command and if they broke the covenant, God would bring trouble on the people and punish them for their sin. This was what had happened. Some of the special things had been stolen.

God then declared, 'Israel will not be able to stand up to their enemies. Tell the people to get up and consecrate themselves. For the LORD God says, "There are devoted things in your midst and you will not be able to defeat your enemies until you take these things away."'

God then told Joshua to gather the people tribe by tribe. And the tribe that the Lord chose would then come out clan by clan. Then the clan that was chosen would come out household by household. And the household chosen by God would come out man by man.

And that man who had stolen the devoted things would be burned with all that he had because he had disobeyed God's special promise.

So Joshua gathered all the tribes. The tribe of Judah was chosen. All the clans of Judah were gathered and the Zerahite clan was chosen. All the families from that clan were gathered and the family of Zabdi was chosen.

Then all the men from the family of Zabdi were gathered together and Achan, the son of Carmi, son of Zabdi was taken.

Joshua pleaded with Achan to give glory to God and to tell the truth. 'Tell me what you have done. Do not hide it from me.'

Achan replied, 'Truly I have sinned against the LORD God of Israel. This is what I did when I saw a beautiful cloak and 200 shekels of silver and a bar of gold. I coveted them and took them. You will find them hidden in the earth inside my tent.'

FACT FILE

Consecrate: To set apart and devote yourself to God.

Covet: To want something that isn't yours.

Joshua sent messengers to Achan's tent where they found the stolen items exactly as Achan had said they would.

Achan's family, who must have realised what Achan had done, were also punished. The whole family was stoned with great stones and Achan was buried there.

It is a tragic story and we can tell how sad the Israelites felt about the whole thing by the name they gave the place where Achan's body lay. It was called 'The Valley of Achor' or 'The Valley of Trouble'.

The LORD said to Joshua, 'Do not fear and do not be dismayed. Take all the fighting men with you and arise. Go up to Ai. I have given into your hand the King of Ai, his people, his city and his land. You shall do to Ai what you did to Jericho. Only its spoil and livestock shall belong to you. Lay an ambush against the city.'

Joshua chose 30,000 men to ambush the city of Ai from behind while he and another 5,000 men would lure the soldiers of Ai out of the main gates. The city of Ai would be left unguarded and therefore be an easy prey for the rest of the army lying in wait.

The main body of the Israelite troops camped on the north side of the city, but no one could see them. The city of Ai did not know they were there. Joshua and the other troops camped on the west and were in full view of the enemy.

When the time for the battle came, Joshua and the 5,000 pretended to be defeated and fled in the direction of the wilderness. The army of Ai set out to pursue them so that not a man was left in the city. Its defences were wide open. God then told Joshua to stretch out his javelin towards Ai. As soon as Joshua did this, the troops hiding north of the city rose up and captured it ... and then they set it ablaze.

When the men of Ai looked back they saw the smoke of the ambushed city rising up to heaven and there was nothing they could do for they were trapped between Joshua and his troop of 5,000 and the 30,000 men ransacking their homes.

No one from the city or the army survived or escaped.

After this victory – Joshua built an altar to the Lord and he read out all of the law of God to the people ... 'the blessing and the curse'. In other words Joshua read out the words of God's law that were written to encourage and strengthen the people ... as well as the words that were written to warn and rebuke them. Joshua read out all the words of the law of God to all the people – both the visitors and the natives, the men and the women – even the very youngest child was there to hear every word that God had commanded.

WARRIOR WAYS

On paper you would have thought that the bigger, stronger army of Israel would have defeated Ai. However, Israel had a traitor in its midst – someone who had deliberately broken God's covenant. Due to Achan's disobedience the Lord had withdrawn his strength and support from them. The Bible tells us many times that it is God who is our strength and our help.

The battles that we face day by day, week by week are often spiritual battles. They are battles against wrong doing, against sin, against evil. We fight battles where we have to make the right decision and not sinful decisions. However, because we are sinners to our very core, we often prefer to make wrong choices. We must fight against this urge to sin. But we cannot fight by ourselves. We don't have the strength. We need God's power.

You might think you are good enough to fight sin on your own. You might think, 'God must be really pleased that he doesn't have to sort me out like he has to with these other sinners.'

Well that's not true. Without God's power, sin and the devil will make a right mess out of puny little sinners like you and me.

We need to take the problem of sin to the only one who can help – the Lord God. His son Jesus Christ is the only one who has defeated sin. He did this on the Cross – when he died instead of sinners, and took the punishment that sinners deserved. Ask God to forgive you for your sins, in

Jesus' name. It's a free gift remember – there's no price tag on salvation.

THINK ABOUT JESUS

Do you remember the name the Israelites gave to Achan's burial place? – The Valley of Achor or the Valley of Trouble.

It was such a sad incident. If you had been there that day you would have known for sure what a terrible thing sin is and that it must be punished.

Sin is terrible. Your sin is terrible. Every day we are guilty of sin and deserving of God's anger.

Does that make you feel sad and hopeless? Perhaps that's what the Israelites felt when they came up with the name 'Valley of Trouble'.

But further on in the Bible there is a verse that gives a hint that hope is not far away from any of us. In Hosea 2:15 God says something wonderful: 'The Valley of Achor will be a door of hope.'

How could a place associated with sin and judgement have anything to do with hope? To answer that we need to go to another place and another death.

Achan's death was a just punishment for sin. At Calvary Jesus was crucified on the cross. There he took the punishment for sin that he had not committed. It is because of what Jesus did that we can have hope of heaven even while we are living in this sinful world.

Read more: You can read about the Battle of Ai in Joshua 7 and 8.

HEZEKIAH'S PRAYER

There are many skills that you need to become a great warrior. In Bible times people wanted good swordsmen, or strong wrestlers or perhaps devious spies.

Which of the following do you think would be useful when fighting a battle?

a. Loads of soldiers?

b. A scary reputation?

c. Clever, crafty plots?

d. Letter writing?

e. Patience?

f. Someone else to fight for you?

Do you think it is strange that letter writing features in this list? Well it does – read on and you'll see.

Hezekiah, the King of Judah, had to face an enemy called Sennacherib, King of Assyria who had both of our first points – loads of soldiers and a scary reputation.

Sennacherib and his father before him had defeated many lands. Every fortress, city and nation that they attacked either surrendered or was totally trashed. And the Kingdom of Judah, the land ruled by the descendants of David, was next on Sennacherib's list. His reputation was so terrifying that Hezekiah tried to buy them off at first by paying Sennacherib with gold. In order to pay all that Sennacherib demanded Hezekiah stripped all the gold from the temple doors. But it was no good, Sennacherib still continued to lay siege to the city of Jerusalem.

When an army lays siege to a city, they surround it on all sides, making sure that no one can get in with supplies and that nobody can get out to fetch help. A siege can go on for a long time and often the city will run out of resources so that the people are weak from lack of food and water. Then the enemy attacks.

Sennacherib had laid siege to many towns and cities and was confident that Jerusalem would be just like all the other cities he had laid waste. Sennacherib was arrogant, mean, cruel and utterly scornful towards the Lord God.

Hezekiah, on the other hand, did what was good, right and faithful before the Lord his God.

So when Sennacherib's army attacked them, Hezekiah did two things – he arranged a crafty plot of his own (point c), but he also encouraged the people to trust in God.

What was the crafty plot? Well if you are an invading army, there is one crucial natural resource you will need to get your hands on – water. There was plenty of water around Jerusalem but Hezekiah did not want the Assyrians to get their hands on it. So he gathered his officers and mighty men and together they came up with a plan to stop the water springs that were outside the city. The people also built up the city defences under Hezekiah's instructions and started to make weapons and shields in abundance. All the people were organized into fighting groups with commanders. Hezekiah then gave his speech.

I'm sure you've heard speeches like this in the movies. Just before the battle begins, the hero of the film rides back and fore in front of his troops, or stands with his spear held high on a podium

– looking straight into the eyes of the anxious warriors preparing for battle. He then calls out to his men to have courage, to be ready to win the battle. 'There's no way we can lose, men. We're so much stronger than our enemy.'

Well Hezekiah did something like this but his words were way better ... they inspired real confidence in the people. Hezekiah spoke encouragingly saying, 'Be strong and courageous. Do not be afraid or dismayed before the King of Assyria and all the horde that is with him. With him is an army of flesh, but with us is the Lord our God, to help us and to fight our battles.'

And the people took confidence from the words of Hezekiah King of Judah.

However, Sennacherib continued to shout insults against Hezekiah and his God. He sent messengers to try and persuade the Israelite people to abandon their fight, their king and their God.

'Have any other gods delivered nations out of the hands of the King of Assyria?' demanded Sennacherib. 'How then can the Lᴏʀᴅ deliver Jerusalem out of my hand?'

Ugh. What a horrible, self-important, obnoxious individual! We can also call him a blasphemer. He was hurling verbal abuse at the one true God – this is called blaspheming or taking the name of the Lord in vain. In the Ten Commandments, God instructs us that this is something we should never do.

But Sennacherib was doing it and he was in fact making a regular habit of it!

However, the prophet Isaiah sent encouraging words to Hezekiah to keep his spirits up – these were words that God had sent to Isaiah – so Hezekiah knew he could trust them.

'Do not be afraid because of the words that you have heard. Behold I will put a spirit in the

King of Assyria. He shall hear a rumour and return to his own land. I will make him fall by the sword in his own land.'

But Sennacherib continued to defy the Lord. This time he sent a letter! ... There I told you letter writing would feature in this story.

Sennacherib sent a very strongly worded letter – designed to strike fear into the heart of the King of Judah.

'Do not let your God in whom you trust deceive you by promising that Jerusalem will not be given into the hand of the King of Assyria. Behold you have heard what the kings of Assyria have done to all lands, devoting them to destruction. And shall you be delivered?

'Like the gods of the nations of the lands who have not delivered their people from my hands so the God of Hezekiah will not deliver his people from my hand.'

Hezekiah read the letter and went up to the house of the Lord and spread it before the Lord. Then Hezekiah prayed.

'O Lord the God of Israel, who is enthroned above the cherubim, you are the God, you alone, of all the kingdoms of the earth. You have made heaven and earth.

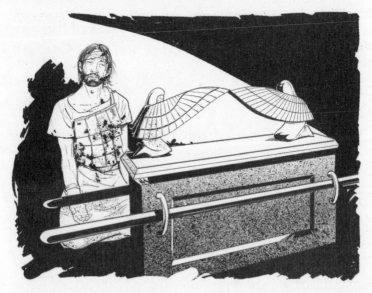

'Incline your ear and hear, O Lord, and hear; open your eyes, O Lord, and see and hear the words of Sennacherib which he has sent to mock the living God.

'Truly O LORD, the kings of Assyria have laid waste the nations and their lands and have cast their gods into the fire, for they were not gods, but the work of men's hands, wood and stone. Therefore they were destroyed. So now, O LORD our God, save us, please from his hand, that all the kingdoms of the earth may know that you, O LORD are God alone.'

So Sennacherib sent a letter to Hezekiah, Hezekiah sent a prayer to God and then God sent a message to Sennacherib through the prophet Isaiah.

Sennacherib had been boasting about all the countries he'd defeated but Isaiah reminded him that everything Sennacherib did was under God's control, everything Sennacherib had done had already been planned by God long ago.

'I know your sitting down and your going out and coming in,' God declared. 'And your raging against me.'

99

God saw it all 'Because of your raging against me ... I will put a hook in your nose and my bit in your mouth and I will turn you back on the way by which you came.'

Just like a horse harnessed with a bit and bridle or a fish caught on a hook – Sennacherib would be forced to go where he didn't want to. And the people of Jerusalem would survive because God had said that they would. Sennacherib wouldn't even shoot an arrow within the city walls.

'For I will defend the city to save it for my own sake for the sake of my servant David,' God proclaimed.

That night the angel of the Lord went out and struck down 185,000 in the Assyrian camp. When the rest of the Assyrian army got up the next morning all they saw was dead bodies. Sennacherib saw this scene of destruction before him and fled straight home.

What a horrifying thing to wake up to. There hadn't been a battle. Everyone had gone to bed and slept soundly – yet by morning thousands of men had died.

Isaiah had said that Sennacherib would hear a rumour and flee. There must have been plenty of rumours doing the rounds that morning in the Assyrian camp ... rumours about what had caused the deaths, who was responsible, why it had happened. Sennacherib must have heard one of these rumours or several of them and in fear he had made his escape.

But the truth was that the destruction had come through the power of the one true God, the one Sennacherib had disregarded and insulted throughout the entire siege.

Do you remember the last part of Isaiah's prophecy? Sennacherib was in fact struck down by the sword in his own land – by his own sons!

WARRIOR WAYS

This story tells us that we need to both trust in God and do what we can. Trusting in God does not mean that we do nothing about the challenges and troubles we face in life. We should do our best to be wise, to work, to obey God's Word. Trusting doesn't mean we sit around doing nothing. When we have difficulties we must pray. We need to ask God for wisdom so that we know what to do. We need to ask God to show us his instructions in his Word. When we trust in God we will actively obey him, communicate with him by prayer, do whatever we can with our mind, body and spirit to give praise and glory to him. When we trust God in our daily battles, we won't be anxious or worried. We will be encouraged by the fact that God is in control of us and our problems – and our enemies.

THINK ABOUT JESUS

It's interesting to see the prophet Isaiah mentioned in this story.

Isaiah lived hundreds of years before Jesus Christ was born, yet many of the words and prophecies of Isaiah came true when Jesus Christ was born and during his life, death and resurrection.

Isaiah's prophecy about Sennacherib came true so look up the following verses to see some of the prophecies Isaiah gave about Jesus Christ that also came true.

Isaiah 7:14; Isaiah 9:6-7; Isaiah 43.

Read more: As well as reading about the defeat of Sennacherib in 2 Kings 18-19, and 2 Chronicles 32 you can read the story again in Isaiah 36–37.

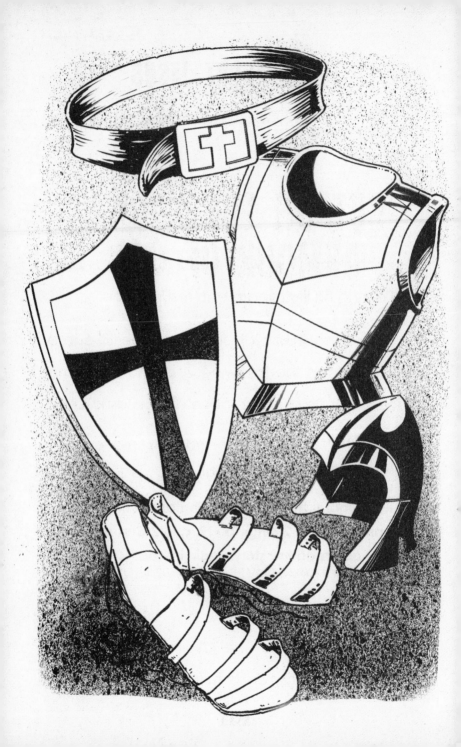

PUT ON THE WHOLE ARMOUR OF GOD

Okay – there are lots of weapons that warriors use. And today we have some weapons that are entirely different to those used hundreds of years ago. For example computers are often used in warfare today – a very different style of fighting to charging across fields on horseback.

But remember, for the Christian believer the battles are not physical battles – they are spiritual ones. Something different again. It's a battle against spiritual powers who want to tempt us away from the Lord God, it's a battle against our sinful nature which prefers to do things for its own sinful pleasure rather than obey God and give him the glory.

So think about that spiritual battle and how you could use the following items as weapons in the fight against evil, and in the fight to give glory to God's name. How can these things be tools for good, to help the church, to spread the gospel?

a. A house

b. A car

c. A pen

d. An education

e. A bank account

There are lots of weapons that God has given us to fight for his kingdom. Every time we obey his Word and give glory to his name, we win a victory with God's help.

One New Testament warrior was the Apostle Paul. He started off as a bitter enemy of Jesus Christ and was passionate about throwing Christians in prison and even killing them.

But God's plans were different and one day, on the road to a city called Damascus, Paul, who was then called Saul, met the Lord Jesus Christ, as a flash of light knocked him from his horse. The Lord spoke directly to him. Paul called out 'Lord, Lord'.

Because the light had blinded him, he had to be led to the home of a Christian for his own safety and to recover. Yet in a strange way Paul could see better than ever. He could see who Jesus really was – the Son of God, the promised Messiah, his Lord and Saviour. Paul, the enemy of Christ, became his follower and someone who would now fight evil by declaring God's Word.

FACT FILE

Messiah: This is the name that the Jewish people used for the one that God had promised to send and save them. Some Jews mistakenly thought the Messiah would be a warrior who would rescue them from the Romans who had invaded their country. However, God's promised Messiah was Jesus Christ who had been sent to save sinners from the punishment of sin. Something far, far greater.

A large part of the New Testament was written by Paul. The New Testament is that part of God's Word that was written after Jesus' death and resurrection and is about Jesus' life and death and the teachings of the apostles such as Matthew, John, Peter and Paul as well as some others.

Paul wrote quite a bit of the New Testament. So you might say that Paul used his pen to fight against evil. But he also spoke to people face to face about the truth of Jesus Christ.

In fact there is a famous speech that Paul made once to a group of educated men in Athens called the Areopagus. The people of Athens worshipped so many different false gods they even had an altar to the 'unknown god'.

So Paul decided to tell them about this unknown God – who was actually the one and only true God – a God not made by human hands like all their other idols.

Paul warned them that God commanded all people everywhere to repent of their sin because a day had been fixed when God would judge the world and that the judge would be Jesus Christ whom God had risen from the dead as proof that all this was true and would happen.

Some of the people who listened that day laughed at Paul. Some simply dismissed his message saying that they'd listen to him again some other time. Others, however, listened and believed.

It was people like this in the different towns and cities that Paul visited who formed what we call the early church. There were congregations in places like Rome, Thessalonica, Philippi, Antioch, Corinth and Ephesus.

Paul used his weapon, the pen, to help the early church fight against the evil of lies that people tried to trick the new Christians with. Paul's letters gave them warnings about these lies and advice about how to live as Christians.

One of the lessons that he gave the Christians in Ephesus is in a New Testament book called Ephesians. Take a look at chapter six verses 10 to 12.

The Whole Armour of God

'Finally, be strong in the Lord and in the strength of his might. Put on the whole armour of God, that you may be able to stand against the schemes of the devil. For we do not wrestle against flesh and blood, but against the rulers, against the authorities, against the cosmic powers over this present darkness, against the spiritual forces of evil in the heavenly places.'

111

What Paul is telling us is that a Christian's worst enemy is not charging down the road waving a sword or shooting a gun at them. A Christian's enemy is the devil and the spiritual forces that follow evil.

However, God has provided his followers with a special armour for defence and protection. Christians are to use this armour – all of it! This armour is what we need to fight against the evil plans that the devil has for us.

The Belt of Truth

"Take up the whole armour of God ... fasten on the belt of truth."

God's Word from Genesis to Revelation is truth. We need to read it and think about it and learn from it. We need to take every opportunity to get strength from the Word of God.

Just as a belt kept all of a soldier's clothes and armour in place so the belt of truth – God's Word – keeps our Christian life in place, it keeps us trusting in and obeying God. If we neglect God's Word, things start falling apart. We will make wrong decisions, we'll start getting confused about what really is the truth and we'll start to believe in lies.

The Breastplate of Righteousness

The next bit of armour we need is the breastplate of Righteousness. The breastplate was the bit of armour that protected the heart of the warrior. In your body your heart is a vital organ and if it is harmed and injured then that spells disaster for the rest of your body. Your heart is a body part that the rest of your body depends on for life.

That's why a soldier's breast plate was such an important piece of armour. The breastplate of righteousness is important in our spiritual battles too. Righteousness is something that we don't have as human beings. We're sinners. We're born that way. God is the one who is righteous. When he looks on us he sees us as sinners – unrighteous. Because we are sinners we must be punished. Sin must be punished.

So how do we get the righteousness that we need to protect us from God's anger? God gives us this righteousness himself. Isn't that amazing! God protects us from himself. He did that by sending his Son to this earth to live and then to die in our place. At the cross of Calvary Jesus took the punishment for our sin and swapped it for his righteousness. He gave those who trust in him the righteousness that they didn't deserve so that when God the father looked on those that his Son had saved all he saw was his Son's righteousness. And when God looked on his Son all he saw was sin – so he punished his Son instead.

If you die without the protection of Christ's righteousness you will be punished by God's anger and this punishment will be eternal. So turn from your sin to the one true God and to Christ our loving Saviour. Put on the breastplate of righteousness.

The Shoes of the Gospel of Peace

An army has to be on its feet a lot. So another important piece of armour are shoes or boots – to protect a soldier's feet. Paul describes  the Christian's shoes as being 'the gospel of peace'.

The gospel is another word for good news – and the good news that Paul tells us about is the good news of Jesus Christ.

Here is the good news of Jesus Christ in some Bible verses:

For God so loved the world that he gave his only Son, that whoever believes in him should not perish but have eternal life (John 3:16).

Believe in the Lord Jesus, and you will be saved, you and your household (Acts 16:31).

For I am sure that neither death nor life, nor angels nor rulers, nor things present nor things to come, nor powers, nor height nor depth, nor anything else in all creation, will be able to separate us from the love of God in Christ Jesus our Lord (Romans 8:38-39).

For while we were still weak, at the right time Christ died for the ungodly ... but God shows his love for us in that while we were still sinners, Christ died for us (Romans 5:6-8).

This good news is essential to keep us marching in the way that God wants us to go. The good news of the gospel is such an important part of our armour. Without the gospel we would have no hope or peace. But the gospel of Jesus Christ gives us a certain hope of heaven and a peace in our hearts – that whatever comes our way we can trust in God.

We might not think of shoes as being armour but without them a soldier would be hopping along the road with blisters and sores – not getting anywhere very fast.

Without the message of the gospel of Christ, a Christian has nothing. Without shoes a soldier should just stay in the barracks – without the good news of Jesus Christ, Christians would have no peace and no hope.

The Shield of Faith

A shield is a piece of armour that protects you from injury and attack. The Christian's shield is called the shield of. Faith. You have to have this gift of faith from God because with it you will 'extinguish all the flaming darts of the evil one.'

117

The evil one is the devil, but what are the flaming darts?

In battles long ago there used to be archers who would take their bows and fire arrows or darts into the opposing army. Sometimes they would set the arrows on fire in order to cause further injury. But if they used their shields they would be able to fend off those fiery darts – and then pour water over them to stop the fire.

In our Christian life we need to trust in God. Faith helps us to do this. What is faith? The Bible tells us: 'Now faith is the assurance of things hoped for, the conviction of things not seen' (Hebrews 11:1).

When we trust and believe in the Lord and his Word we will have faith and confidence that God is real. We can't see him but we will have faith in his power and his truth and his justice. We will believe that God sent his Son, Jesus Christ, to take the punishment for our sin. We will believe that eternal life is his free gift to us and that nothing can separate us from his love; nothing can defeat our Lord God. We will have faith that with his armour and his strength we are on the winning side. Whenever the Devil tries to confuse us or make us doubt God, we can use God's gift of faith to squash these doubts.

Do you want faith? Ask God for it. He is the only one who can give you this faith and it is through faith in Christ Jesus that we are saved.

The Helmet of Salvation

Next to your heart, your head is probably the most important part of your body. If either your heart or head is seriously hurt you are in danger of losing your life. That's why  you wear a helmet when you cycle or go rock climbing. The helmet protects your head and the important organ – your brain – that is inside it. So the helmet is an important piece of armour for a soldier.

What is the most important thing for a Christian? It is what Jesus did on the cross. Jesus died to save us from sin – he died to give us forgiveness of sin – this is called Salvation. Because he took the punishment for sin by dying in the place of sinners those who trust in Christ have been freed from sin's punishment for ever. They have been forgiven for their sins. Believers can trust that one day in heaven they will be without sin and will enjoy eternal life. This is all because of the salvation that Jesus Christ achieved for his people on the cross.

Without salvation there would be everlasting punishment. So put on the helmet of salvation – trust in Jesus Christ.

The Sword

Our final piece of armour has a different purpose. All the other parts

of the armour have been defensive... but this time we have a sword. A sword is used to attack with. And just as the belt was used to describe God's Word so is the sword.

How is the Bible like a sword? How do we use it to fight God's enemies? Well, sometimes we will be in situations where we hear people speak lies against God and his Word. This is why we need to study God's Word so that we can stand up against those lies. We need to tell the enemies of God what God's Word says so that they can hear it and believe and be saved. Some won't believe it, but we still have to tell them the truth.

So put God's armour on and keep it on. Don't let things slip. Put on the whole armour of God and you will be strong in the Lord and in the strength of his might.

Read more: You can read about the whole armour of God in Ephesians 6:10-20.

SO ARE YOU A BIBLE WARRIOR?

What have we learned from these true stories from the Bible?

1. We've learned that God is Sovereign. That's another word which means God is in control.

2. We've seen that victories and defeats are all part of God's plan.

3. God's Word teaches us that every day is a battle against temptation, sin and evil.

4. We've learned that we cannot fight these spiritual battles in our own strength. We need God's power.

5. In the Bible we see that there are only two sides in the spiritual battle – God's side and Satan's side.

6. God's side is the winning side. Jesus defeated sin and death at the cross.

7. Although people who trust in Jesus are still tempted to sin, the war against sin has been won. Christ's death and resurrection prove this.

8. Every battle that is won against sin, every victory in our personal lives is done with God's help.

9. In everything we must give the glory to God.

10. Read the Bible and pray.

11. Trust in Jesus Christ to save you from sin. He will continue to work in your life until that day comes when you go to heaven to be with him – sinless, forever.

WHO IS
THE AUTHOR?

Let me introduce myself. My name is Catherine Mackenzie and I live in Inverness, in the Highlands of Scotland.

From a very early age I have loved books and stories. One day as a child the only way my parents could persuade me to take my medicine was to promise me a book. So I took a deep breath and swallowed.

Even as a child I knew that I wasn't really a Christian. I knew I didn't love Jesus in the same way as the woman who washed Jesus' feet with her tears. But several years after I read that story for the first time I realised that I needed God's forgiveness through Jesus Christ, his Son.

These days the kid who loved to read now loves to write. The idea for this book, How to Be a *Bible Warrior*, came because I wanted boys to read a book that would encourage them to be men of God; something that would help them realise that God is the most important person in everyone's story. The descriptions of warriors in the Bible are not just about exciting heroes. These stories are there to teach us about God – and how he is the real hero.

I hope this book will help young boys to grow up to be men who will glorify God and enjoy him forever.

Muscles and physical toughness are not the main characteristics of a true warrior. What I love about this book is that it shows us that true warriors are truth warriors who honour God no matter the difficulties they face. They are spiritually strong because they take their strength from Christ. Devour this book to help build your spiritual muscles so that you too can be a truth warrior.

Stewart Mackay
Army Chaplain
British Armed Forces

BOOKS BY IRENE HOWAT

Books were amongst some of the things set alight during church history. In fact, flames were used to persecute Christians throughout church history.

Irene Howat tells the Christian story behind some amazing historical incidents. You will see how not even fire, or the plans of evil men, can separate Christians from the love of God.

ISBN: 978-1-84550-781-7

God used fire to get Moses to pay attention and to help the Israelites find their way through the dark. Jesus himself cooks a fish barbie on the beach after his resurrection and the Holy Spirit comes down on the disciples at Pentecost with tongues of flame.

ISBN: 978-1-84550-780-0